ever

faith

**Reflections and prayers to help you
find and follow God in everyday life**

Nick Shepherd, Mark Greene and Rachel Treweek

CHURCH HOUSE
PUBLISHING

Published 2019 by Church House Publishing
www.chpublishing.co.uk

Church House Publishing, Church House, Great Smith Street, London SW1P 3AZ

© The Archbishops' Council of the Church of England 2019

ISBN 978 1 78140 139 2 (Single Copy)
ISBN 978 1 78140 140 8 (10-Pack)

We are grateful to all those who have given permission for us to share their stories. Please note that some names have been changed on request.

We acknowledge and greatly thank the London Institute for Contemporary Christianity (LICC) who provided all but one of the stories of everyday faith in this booklet, including three abridged from *The One About…* by Mark Greene (LICC, 2018). We are grateful to the Diocese of London for 'The one about minding the gap'. The copyright for LICC's stories remains with LICC. For more information on the work of LICC, visit **www.licc.org.uk**

Prayers on pp. 9–15 from *Common Worship: Services and Prayers for the Church of England* and *New Patterns for Worship* are copyright © The Archbishops' Council 2000–2008 and are published by Church House Publishing. Used here with permission.

Scripture quotations are from the New Revised Standard Version of the Bible, Anglicized Edition, copyright © 1989, 1995 by the Division of Christian Education of the National Council of the Churches of Christ in the USA. Used by permission. All rights reserved.

The opinions expressed in this book are those of the authors.

Concept and design by RF Design (UK) Limited

Printed in the UK by Ashford Colour Press

Everyday Faith has been produced by Church House Publishing and the Archbishops' Council's Digital and Setting God's People Free teams. We are grateful to the many members of staff of the National Church Institutions that have made this booklet possible.

Digital and Setting God's People Free are part of the Church of England's Renewal and Reform programme, aimed at helping us become a growing Church for all people and all places. For more information, visit **www.churchofengland.org/about/renewal-reform**

Contents

Foreword

In a B&Q store a regional sales rep for Bosch gathered those whose job was specifically to sell power tools. He began with a question, "What are we in the business of?"

The youngest shop worker, eager to be seen and heard, quickly jumped in, "We are in the business of selling drills."

"No," the sales rep firmly responded, "No, we are not. We are in the business of putting holes in walls."

What is the business of the church?

Of course you could be forgiven for thinking – like that young shop worker – we are simply in the business of getting people to be involved in church or in what we do. But we aren't.

We are in the business of seeing the difference God wants to bring in the whole world.

This is why I am delighted to commend this **Everyday Faith** booklet.

Because its aim is to do just that – to help every follower of Jesus to live out their faith in everyday life. God sends us as God's church to live out our faith in a variety of places and to share the hope and love we have with the people we meet in everyday life.

We are all involved in God's mission – empowered by the Holy Spirit to bring the difference Jesus makes. Because mission isn't something the church runs – but something each of us are involved in. We do this by following Jesus and being his witnesses. This call by Jesus himself makes life an adventure.

I encourage you to take time for the three weeks of this brilliantly written material to allow God's Holy Spirit to inspire, equip and excite you to live your everyday life for him. For the sake of all God wants to do in the world.

+ Just

Archbishop Justin Welby

How to use this book

For now we see in a mirror, dimly, but then we will see face to face. Now I know only in part; then I will know fully, even as I have been fully known. And now faith, hope, and love abide, these three; and the greatest of these is love.

1 Corinthians 13.12–13

The next 21 days are a journey of reflection and prayer. We are probably all aware that being followers of Jesus isn't confined to church activities. Most of us will pray or think about our faith at some point during our waking or working day. The reflections, stories and prayers here are offered to help us discover more about what it means to live faithfully, hopefully and lovingly as Christians today.

Each reflection starts with a Bible passage, with some thoughts on how this links to faith, hope or love in our everyday life. Alongside this is a simple pattern of prayer (see pp. 9–15): a prayer to start the day, a breaktime prayer to pause and reset during the day, and an "examen" prayer for the end of the day to notice where God has been in your day. The reflections connect with stories of how others have found God at work in their lives – real people who have shared with us their story of God's leadings. You can find additional material and animations of these stories online at **www.churchofengland.org/everydayfaith**

The first week's reflections on Faith are written by **Nick Shepherd**. Going to church is a vital part of a living faith, but so is going to work or school, going to the gym, going to friends for coffee, or helping a community project. God is present in our daily lives and faith rests on finding ways to connect with God more fully in our day-to-day lives.

In week 2, **Mark Greene** offers reflections on Hope. The challenge here is to recognise how our everyday faith is shaped by the hope we place in Christ. Part of this rests on grasping that the hope of the Good News is a transforming vision for the whole of creation. We are each called to place our hope in God's transforming activity and to join in with this wherever He places us.

Lastly, **Rachel Treweek** offers reflections on Love. Faith and Hope lead us to Love – the core virtue of our faith. Faith in everyday life is fulfilled by the way in which we allow God's love to work in us and through us.

Everyday Faith Prayers

Your journey through #EverydayFaith will be rooted in prayer. Where and how you use these prayers is up to you. It will depend on whether you are woken at 5 a.m. by a crying baby, or at 6 p.m. by an alarm clock before a night shift. The next few pages give you some ways to start, pause, and end each day by asking, noticing, and reflecting upon where you find God in your everyday life. Whenever you use these prayers, we do encourage you to try to establish a pattern of praying them at similar times each day.

Prayers to start each day

Start the day looking for God in your everyday life.
Use this prayer in the morning, first thing after waking
with a cup of tea, taking time over breakfast, walking
to school, waiting for a bus to work or wherever your
day is about to take you.

GIVE THANKS FOR A NEW DAY

As we rejoice in the gift of this new day,
so may the light of your presence, O God,
set our hearts on fire with love for you;
now and for ever.
Amen.

REFLECT ON GOD'S PRESENCE WITH YOU

God is with you, wherever you may be and whatever
you may choose to do. When might you most need
to keep this in mind?

Creator God,
you made us all in your image:
may we discern you in all that we see,
and serve you in all that we do;
through Jesus Christ our Lord.
Amen.

PRAY THAT CHRIST MAY BE REVEALED

Offer to God the places of your day, the people you will meet, and the ways you will spend your time, that God may be glorified, and Christ revealed, in all you are and all that you do.

**Christ be with me, Christ within me,
Christ behind me, Christ before me,
Christ beside me, Christ to win me,
Christ to comfort and restore me.
Christ beneath me, Christ above me,
Christ in quiet, Christ in danger,
Christ in hearts of all that love me,
Christ in mouth of friend and stranger.
Amen.**

Prayers in the midst of everyday life

*Use one or both of these brief "pauses" during the day.
Give thanks for the blessings you have received and take
a moment to be aware of God in what you are doing.*

THE BLESSINGS OF LIFE

**God is good
all the time.
All the time
God is good.**

**O Lord, you have searched me out and known me;
you know my sitting down and my rising up; you
discern my thoughts from afar. You mark out my
journeys and my resting place and are acquainted
with all my ways.
Amen.**

Psalm 139.1–2

**Lord of creation,
whose glory is around and within us:
open our eyes to your wonders,
that we may serve you with reverence
and know your peace at our lives' end,
through Jesus Christ our Lord.
Amen.**

THANKFULNESS IN BUSYNESS

Lord, you are ever watchful
and bless us with your gifts;
as you provide for all our needs,
so help us to build only what pleases you,
through Jesus Christ our Lord.
Amen.

Unless the Lord builds the house, those who build
it labour in vain. Unless the Lord keeps the city,
the guard keeps watch in vain.

Psalm 127.1–2

Lord Jesus Christ, we thank you
for all the benefits that you have won for us,
for all the pains and insults
that you have borne for us.
Most merciful redeemer,
friend and brother,
may we know you more clearly,
love you more dearly,
and follow you more nearly,
day by day.
Amen.

Evening prayer: God in our every day

Many Christians use a special "examen" (a Latin word for "a means of examining") at the end of the day. An examen has six simple steps:

Find a place to be still
Wherever you are, sit comfortably and be still. Relax, but try to be attentive to yourself and to God.

Give thanks for the good things of today
Recall one moment from the past day that you are grateful for. Remember how you felt. Notice these feelings and reflect that all good things come from God. Offer your thanks.

Let go of things bothering you
What's on your mind at the moment? What is making you feel awkward or anxious? Raise these things to God and ask for the freedom that comes with the presence of the Holy Spirit.

Review your day
Try to recall the other events of the day. Reflect on what has happened and how you feel about it. Trust the Holy Spirit to show you the things that are important to think through and the insights that are important to know.

Talk with God

Tell God anything that comes to mind – jot it down, speak it out or think it through. God already knows our needs, so this is to help us identify what we need to be aware of, let go or recognize.

Finish your prayer

An examen prayer can take a few minutes or a good hour. However long you have been able to give, offer this time to God with a closing prayer.

Before the ending of the day,
Creator of the world, we pray
That you, with steadfast love, would keep
Your watch around us while we sleep.

From evil dreams defend our sight,
From fears and terrors of the night;
Tread underfoot our deadly foe
That we no sinful thought may know.

O Father, that we ask be done
Through Jesus Christ, your only Son;
And Holy Spirit, by whose breath
Our souls are raised to life from death.
Amen.

Living
faith-fully in
everyday life

Reflections by Nick Shepherd

Day 1

An invitation to everyday faith

READING

"Christ is the image of the invisible God, the firstborn of all creation; for in him all things in heaven and on earth were created, things visible and invisible, whether thrones or dominions or rulers or powers – all things have been created through him and for him. He himself is before all things, and in him all things hold together."

Colossians 1.15–17

REFLECTION

Our daily lives are often very full. Full of places to be. Full of people to meet, things to do. For some, they may be full of time on our hands. Full of the hopes we would like to fulfil, things we don't want to face.

How do we find God in the fullness of life, and how in our every day do we find full-ness – abundance – of life? These reflections are designed to help us explore what our faith, our trust in Christ, means to us, and how we live this out in the whole of our lives. The beliefs we hold are a core part of our faith, but faith is also a lived experience. There are points in life when we notice a need to rely on God more than at other times. The good news is that God is with us all the time, not only in crisis moments.

Today's reading from Colossians underlines this. Faith is connecting with the God who holds all things together. So, faith is found in our joys and cares, in our challenges and conflicts as we lean into God's presence and guidance. Faith informs our thinking and our actions as we discern how God might be using us in his work. Faith is an ongoing encounter with God. Faith is our everyday existence with the God who holds all things together.

RESPONSE

Take a moment to reflect on the fullness of your life.

Jot down areas of life that come to mind where you want to experience the fullness of God with you.

the one about...
Victoria's secret

Victoria is an apprentice hairdresser. She's 19 and she's been in the job just over a month. It's a busy salon so there's always something to do and it's almost always got to be done quickly. She's enjoying it – the people are upbeat, friendly – but she's been feeling the pressure. Three weeks into the job, and her vicar prays for her as part of commissioning her for this role.

Commissioned to wash people's hair? What difference does being a Christian make to the way you wash someone's hair? I wonder what you might say if someone asked you what difference does being a Christian make. When asked this question, Victoria didn't miss a beat: "I pray for them as I massage in the conditioner."

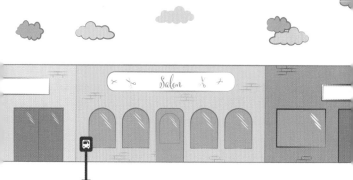

Victoria's praying is an invisible gift to her clients –
soothing conditioner for the soul, not just the hair.
Learning the pressure points that relax individual
clients. Offering points for prayer for each individual
created by God. Still, behind her actions lie a whole
set of beliefs.

Victoria believes that her work – in a hairdressing salon
– is important to God. And why shouldn't she? Isn't God
present in all places? She knows that whatever she
does she can do for God (Colossians 3.17) and that this
work can be done in a distinctive way, that massaging
in conditioner into someone's scalp is a way to bless
someone, a way to love her neighbour as herself
(Matthew 22.39).

Victoria believes in the power of prayer and in God's
freedom to respond in the way that God chooses. She
doesn't need to see the results of those prayers. But
it's still worth praying – God will be listening to her. ●

Day 2

Everyday faith, ordinary actions

READING

"Whatever your task, put yourselves into it, as done for the Lord and not for your masters, since you know that from the Lord you will receive the inheritance as your reward; you serve the Lord Christ."

Colossians 3.23–24

REFLECTION

A remarkable thing happened the other day. When my teenage kids were told that they had haircuts after school they both grunted with enthusiasm. "What, with Nat … ? Great, I like Nat!" Then they chatted away as Nat snipped away. No complaints and more conversation than I get out of them all week!

Our first story of everyday faith is about Victoria. Victoria is a hairdresser and sees this as a vocation. She cuts hair not just for the money, not only for the satisfaction of being creative, not even for the genuine pride found in using her skills to help people feel good;

but because she sees how God can work through her to bless others.

We all have a variety of roles to fulfil. We might feel strongly that one or more of these roles is our vocation. When we think of vocation, we might assume that this only applies to being a priest or to a select type of job, like being a nurse. Someone once described vocation as being where "our talents meet the needs of the world". It might just be that in some of the responsibilities that come in everyday life we can feel this connection. All Christians are called to serve God in God's world and the many roles we already have can be part of this.

This is what Victoria found in her role at work. That's her secret, not just praying blessings on the people she serves.

RESPONSE

How might God use you to bless others today?

What prayers of blessing can you offer as you hit "Send", clean dishes or fit fuse boxes?

Day 3

Faith is a curious thing

READING

*"Moses was keeping the flock of his father-in-law
Jethro, the priest of Midian; he led his flock beyond the
wilderness, and came to Horeb, the mountain of God.
There the angel of the Lord appeared to him in a flame
of fire out of a bush; he looked, and the bush was blazing,
yet it was not consumed. Then Moses said, 'I must turn
aside and look at this great sight, and see why the bush
is not burned up.' When the Lord saw that he had turned
aside to see, God called to him out of the bush, 'Moses,
Moses!' And he said, 'Here I am.' "*

Exodus 3.1–4

REFLECTION

When Moses notices the burning bush, he is busy
doing something else. However, it was probably not
unusual to see a bush on fire in that parched land.
A lightning strike from a storm could set off such a fire
as we see in forest fires today. That wasn't what
Moses noticed, it was the curious fact that the bush
wasn't being burned up. That was what woke him

up to the fact that God was present in that place at that moment.

I wonder if we often talk ourselves out of sensing God's presence in our everyday life. As the author Barbara Brown-Taylor says, most often we can put it down to having too much caffeine, or that there are "more important" things to think about. Why? Why don't we daydream a little more and wake up to God being around us in our every day?

Yet, like a good cup of coffee (or a cold shower if you prefer), we sometimes need a bit of a stimulus to wake up to God in our everyday lives. For Victoria, this involved being asked a challenging question on what difference being a Christian makes to washing someone's hair. I wonder what it was that got her curious, interested in where God might be present? I wonder what you might say to the same question?

RESPONSE

Is there some "little thing" you do in a way that consciously involves God? What might that thing be in how you undertake the roles in your life?

the one about...
No. 10

Mike is sitting in a room with 14 other men, all from the same church. Richard, the group leader, has just asked them this question – "What are you good at 'in the Lord' at work?" A slightly jargony way of putting it, but nevertheless a good question about our gifts and how God might be using us. As if sensing a reticence to talk about something they're good at (especially linked to faith), Richard suggests each person might like to write something down on a post-it note. "Who's first to share?" he then ventures.

Mike is the first. He speaks quietly, tentatively really. "As some of you know, I am a policeman. I'm part of the armed protection team. At Number 10."

He had the attention of the room at "armed protection".

"It's a pretty macho group of people and over the years there's been quite a lot of conflict. And I've found that I am pretty good at bringing people back together."

That's all he says. And then he looks down at the coffee table in front of him. There's a pause – not long enough to be awkward, but definitely a pause. And then someone says, "You've got a ministry of reconciliation." A smile stretches across Mike's face in recognition of this insight. Then someone else says, "Yes, you're a peacemaker." Which of course he is, not only in protecting people but in his team as well. "Blessed are the peacemakers, for they will be called children of God" (Matthew 5.9). And here the group begin to unpack what it might mean to be people who show others what Jesus' message of forgiveness is all about.

Mike had a sense that he had been doing something good but seeing this through the lens of the Bible showed him something else. God was working through him. Through *him*. Being Mike. ●

Day 4

Faith as virtues, not duty

READING

"Jesus said, 'You are the light of the world. A city built on a hill cannot be hidden. No one after lighting a lamp puts it under the bushel basket, but on the lampstand, and it gives light to all in the house. In the same way, let your light shine before others, so that they may see your good works and give glory to your Father in heaven.' "

Matthew 5.14–16

REFLECTION

Every day you will probably notice police on duty – guarding locations, undertaking crowd control at sporting events, responding to traffic accidents and any number of other incidents. Not all stories about our police are positive, but it would be hard to disagree that on the whole we're glad that they are there – doing their duty.

Mike is an armed response officer. A high-pressure role. As a Christian, Mike understands that he needs to fulfil this duty in a manner that reflects his faith. What does this look like for Mike?

Mike's job – his vocation, maybe – is to keep the peace, but Mike has noticed that his duties are not the only way he is a peacemaker. Mike is often the person who will calm down an argument at work. The kind of colleague who won't hold a grudge. Working this out has helped him to notice God at work through him in his everyday life.

It's hard sometimes to picture what the coming Kingdom of heaven looks like. This is where the picture language Jesus uses in the parables helps. The Kingdom is like salt that adds flavour, a small shining light seen from far off, like yeast invisibly working, treasure we stumble across.

RESPONSE

We all have roles we can appreciate as service: as a friend, parent or sibling, as a tenant support worker, crucial supply chain link, baker or banker ... What is it about you, about the way that God is forming you, that really shines?

Day 5

Faith as joining up and joining in

READING

"The spirit of the Lord God is upon me, because the Lord has anointed me; he has sent me to bring good news to the oppressed, to bind up the broken-hearted, to proclaim liberty to the captives, and release to the prisoners; to proclaim the year of the Lord's favour … to provide for those who mourn in Zion – to give them a garland instead of ashes, the oil of gladness instead of mourning."

Isaiah 61.1–3

REFLECTION

I remember once having a conversation with a police officer who was part of my church. She had had a really hard week as part of a team investigating a particularly awful crime. She was pleased to have fellow Christians with which to share how this experience of sin – very real sin – had not only affected the victims of this crime, but her as well. Taking a stand against the wrongs in the world is tough going – even if we are not faced with situations as difficult as this.

Our trust in living faithfully is that God is establishing the kingdom through what Jesus has done to defeat sin, and through the ongoing work of the Spirit. This is a transformation, however, that we are called to participate in. Following Christ in everyday life involves taking a stand, or a stance, towards seeking a world shaped by the values of this kingdom. The Christian writer John Pritchard suggests this will involve "constantly turning our lives towards God as a sunflower constantly turns its face to the sun".

We grow in confidence and joy when other Christians help us see and celebrate what God is doing in and through us. How our small stands make a difference. This can be as simple as asking each other questions, or as profound as sharing our vulnerabilities.

RESPONSE
What has God been showing you recently about how he is working through you?
Why not share this with a friend or group.
Why not ask them what they think as well.

the one about...
the travelling Trenemans

Gary and Amahle Treneman do quite a lot of their travelling by bus. They've got to that age where it's free and anyway they don't own a car. Besides, it's always a bit of an adventure. Not because life has got so dull that standing in the pouring rain waiting for the 141 is the highlight of their week but because, well, they never know what might happen.

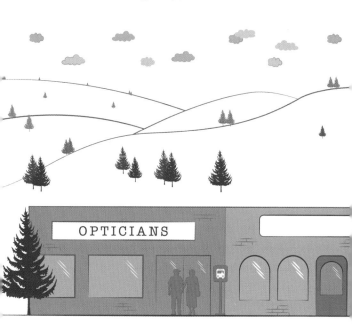

OPTICIANS

Just last week they were on the 288 coming back from the opticians. Amahle sat down next to a woman who started talking to her. She was, according to Gary, "quite young really, only about 78". As it happened they got off at the same stop and Amahle said to her, "We are Christians and before we leave home, we ask God to guide us to people. We don't stand on the street corner handing out booklets, but if a person starts a conversation with us we always like to offer one that talks about God's love." The "young" woman beamed at her, and gave her a big hug. And Amahle asked her name so she could pray for her.

Of course, God doesn't limit the adventure of following nudges to their travelling. On one occasion, Amahle was itching to leave work and get home but she sensed a nudging to go to the canteen. Over the years she's learned to recognize this as God's prompting – the shepherd's voice (John 10.27). While sipping a cup of tea, she heard someone crying some way behind her. She went over and introduced herself to Kiera, a young woman of about 19. This was the first of many conversations. Kiera is now a follower of Jesus. Whether it's a walk to the canteen or a hop round the corner, every journey can be a mission trip. ●

Day 6

Freedom to live faith-fully

READING

"When the Spirit of truth comes, he will guide you into all the truth; for he will not speak on his own, but will speak whatever he hears, and he will declare to you the things that are to come."

John 16.13

REFLECTION

Gary and Amahle have got a freedom pass, and they're not afraid to use it. The chance to travel to new, or familiar, places is something that they relish. The opportunity to chat to new, and familiar, friends is a bonus of this adventurous spirit. They use this freedom to the full.

The Trenemans are living examples of the journey being the destination. As they travel on the buses they have opened this part of everyday life up as an adventure to take with God. They have learned to be open to God nudging them to speak or respond to the people they meet. Often with just a greeting or a smile but always with an openness to talk.

Sometimes it can be easy for us to forget that God is often active in the everyday life of other people. It helps to be a little bit more curious about what God might be up to. Even if we can't see ourselves being as adventurous as the Trenemans, we can nudge ourselves to be nudged by God a little more. Sometimes this role is listening and learning. On the buses, in the school grounds, in the canteen … wherever we journey.

RESPONSE

What might make something you often do a bit more of an adventure? Where is God nudging you to see an invitation to journey with the Spirit as your guide?

Day 7

Faithful guidance

READING

"Then the Lord called, 'Samuel! Samuel!' and he said, 'Here I am!' and ran to Eli, and said, 'Here I am, for you called me.' … Then Eli perceived that the Lord was calling the boy. Therefore Eli said to Samuel, 'Go, lie down; and if he calls you, you shall say, "Speak, Lord, for your servant is listening." ' So Samuel went and lay down in his place."

1 Samuel 3.4–5, 8–9

REFLECTION

In The Book of Common Prayer, the prayer of Confirmation spoken by the Bishop is for the daily increase in "gifts of grace; the spirit of wisdom and understanding; the spirit of counsel and ghostly strength; the spirit of knowledge and true godliness". Confirmation reminds us that we are called to be disciples in the power of the Holy Spirit – not in our own strength. Though trusting in the presence of the Holy Spirit requires a bit of ghostly strength!

Hearing God's voice isn't easy. The Trenemans' story
is one founded in decades of practice. When God
spoke to Samuel, he didn't recognize this at first.
It took Eli to share his wisdom for this to make sense.

Similarly for us God's leading comes to us mingled
with our own thoughts, desires and feelings. It's always
a good idea to seek wisdom from others, especially
in significant decisions. However, here we're thinking
about those nudges and promptings that happen
throughout the day. Maybe we could trust these
a little more – especially if they prompt actions that,
while they might put us out a bit, are the types of
gestures of interest and kindness we might all like
to receive from time to time.

RESPONSE
Using the "examen" evening prayer today
(see p.14), reflect on this week's journey and
the ways in which you are becoming more
attuned to God's voice. Note these
and discuss them with a trusted friend.

Living everyday faith hopefully

WEEK 2

Reflections by Mark Greene

Day 8

Hope in Sunday's promise

READING

*"The mother of Jesus said to him, 'They have no wine.' …
Jesus said to the servants, 'Fill the jars with water'
… When the steward tasted the water that had become
wine … he called the bridegroom and said to him,
'Everyone serves the good wine first … But you have
kept the good wine until now.' "*

John 2.3, 7, 9–10

REFLECTION

Hope in the Bible isn't wishful thinking. It's the
certainty both that there is a new heaven and a new
earth to look forward to, and that all that happens
to us now will, by God's grace, be turned to good.
The certainty of a glorious future puts the present
in perspective.

But there's more.

Jesus' kingdom has broken in and so new possibilities
abound now, foretastes of what is to come: divine

interventions, providential "coincidences", messages from above, prayers answered.

Jesus' first miracle is both a generous gift of 900 bottles of wine and a foretaste of the great wedding banquet of Christ and his bride, the Church. The wine Jesus made was better than what had been served before, just as our life in him in eternity will be better than anything we have yet tasted.

A day of rest is similar. A Sabbath rest – Sunday or not – is intended to be a reminder and a foretaste of that greater rest to come. A sign to the world of a different possibility. And our everyday lives among our friends, our families, our colleagues are also intended to be a sign: with Christ, there is a different way. The hope alive in us is a pointer to the hope for them.

RESPONSE

Sabbath is about looking back as well as looking forward. Think about the past week: where have you seen God at work in your life? Or the lives of others? What tokens of his love have you noticed? What are you grateful for?

the one about...
the dogs

The helicopter pilot had radioed ahead so they knew she was coming in. Joan, mid-40s, a farmer, arm dangling off after an encounter with a chainsaw. Gabi, the head nurse, hugely experienced, a trainer of emergency nurses, would lead the triage team.

Joan is wheeled in – losing lots of blood, pulse high, blood pressure plummeting, breathing erratic. There are two priorities: keep her alive;

try to save the arm. Gabi had seen scores of patients in comparable high-jeopardy situations and they are usually very compliant with the medical team – they do exactly what they are told, they answer questions quickly, they focus. Curiously, Joan seems preoccupied, her mind elsewhere. Gabi is puzzled. She prays, "Why Lord?" God says, "Ask her."

So Gabi asks a woman whose arm is dangling off, with a high pulse, plummeting blood pressure and erratic breathing what seems like an absurd question: "Joan, what else is going on for you at the moment?" And Joan says, "No one can look after my dogs tonight." Her arm is dangling off but she's worried about her dogs. Gabi says, "We'll sort that," and tells a nurse to get a message to Joan's emergency contact. Immediately, Joan's blood pressure rises, her pulse goes down, and her breathing stabilizes.

Joan lived. And the team saved her arm.

And the dogs were fed.

When the times get tough – and when they aren't – ask God in. ●

Day 9

Hope for Monday

READING

"The Lord God planted a garden in Eden ... and there he put the man whom he had formed ... The Lord God took the man and put him in the garden of Eden to till it and keep it."

Genesis 2.8, 15

REFLECTION

Hopelessness comes in many forms: the anguish of grief, loss, betrayal, the despair that this situation will never get better. Still, one of the quieter, more corrosive forms of hopelessness is the secret sense that the things we do day by day – the data entry, the three loads of washing, the e-mails – don't really matter to God. And if they don't matter, aren't I just wasting my time?

But, as today's reading shows us, work is a big part of what God created us to do. God's work of creation in Genesis produces order, provides food, generates joy, creates beauty, gives people the opportunity to develop the potential of his creation, for his glory and the benefit of others. Similarly, our daily work is intended to imitate God's in contributing to making our bit of the world more like the way God would like it to be. For God's glory.

So, doing the washing creates order, prevents disease, brings joy to the wearers – and perhaps a greater measure of beauty – and liberates them to do whatever God has given them to do that day. And those are all things that are utterly in line with God's purposes. Our work matters to God, even down to ensuring a dog gets fed.

RESPONSE

Jot down some of the tasks you are going to do today. Who will benefit? How will it contribute to making your bit of the world a bit better?

Ask God for the wisdom and strength to do whatever you do in his way and to his glory.

Day 10

Hope in the crisis

READING

"When the captains of the chariots saw Jehoshaphat, they said, 'It is the king of Israel.' So they turned to fight against him; and Jehoshaphat cried out, and the Lord helped him. God drew them away from him ..."

2 Chronicles 18.31

REFLECTION

Pressure moments often reveal our instincts. Where do we turn? What or who do we turn to?

Gabi, the nurse, realizes that there was something going on beyond her professional expertise to deal with. She prays. Jehoshaphat, surrounded in a battle he should not have been in, is not so gripped by fear in the moment that he cannot think to cry out to God.

The challenges we face on our frontlines, the places where God calls us to live out our faith in our daily lives, may not be matters of life and death. We might not all have roles like Gabi's. Yet we do all encounter people in crisis – the child that just loses it in the classroom, the boss that bawls us out for no apparent reason, the colleague we can hear weeping in the loo, the car crash that happens just in front of us … We can't predict the crises, we can't necessarily prepare. But there is hope in the moment. Cry out to God, the one who sees all, knows all.

RESPONSE

Think about a pressure moment you've been through in the past. How did you respond? What was good? What would you like to do differently? Ask God for grace to turn to him for help in the pressure moments that inevitably will come to you in the future.

the one about...
the boy
unmentioned

Adrian has retired from full-time teaching, but he does some supply work in secondary schools.

Like many a teacher, when he's set the pupils some work, he often walks up and down the class, pausing here and there at a desk. No doubt the pupils think he is glancing over their work. No doubt sometimes he is. But often he's praying for them by name. It takes something to do that, doesn't it? To remember that God loves every one of these people, that God answers prayer, and to pray and trust him for the answers, even though he is very unlikely to see any difference himself, or be able to tell anyone else that something amazing has happened …

One day, like any other day, Adrian is in a class of 14-year-olds. He's set them some work. He walks up and down the class. He stops by one of the boys and begins to pray. And then he hears God say this to him: "No one has ever mentioned this boy's name to me before."

Imagine that. No one has ever mentioned this boy's name to God before. No health visitor prayed for him, no lollipop person, no doctor, no primary school teacher, no football coach, no sweetshop owner, no bus driver, no schoolfriend … no one.

But God is listening – waiting, it seems, alert at that moment to the fact that at last someone lifted this person to his throne. Delighted.

God hears every prayer. God cares for every person. And your prayer for some person may be the only one anyone prays.

Only when Jesus returns will we get to see how he has worked through the things we regard as little things, and created, we hope and trust, something gloriously beautiful. ●

Day 11

Hope – right where we are

READING

"Then Jacob woke from his sleep and said, 'Surely the Lord is in this place – and I did not know it!' And he was afraid, and said, 'How awesome is this place! This is none other than the house of God, and this is the gate of heaven.' "

Genesis 28.16–17

REFLECTION

Sometimes we can fall into the trap of believing that God isn't really interested in the places we spend our Monday-to-Saturday lives: our workplaces, our gyms, our shops, our clubs. We can suppose that we could be much more fruitful for him somewhere else other than at this desk, or this checkout, or this school gate. But where we are, God is – as God confirmed to Adrian in that classroom.

Jacob has stolen his brother Esau's birthright and is fleeing for his life. At nightfall, he beds down in the hills with a stone for a pillow. God appears to him in a dream, promising, "I am with you and will keep you wherever you go, and will bring you back to this land." When he wakes, Jacob acknowledges God's presence and thinks of this place as particularly special – the gate of heaven – and names it Bethel, house of God.

But Jacob was wrong. It wasn't that God dwelled in that particular spot a few miles north of Jerusalem, it was that God made Jacob aware of his presence there. God is with us wherever we are. That's the promise. And therein lies the hope: where God is, possibilities abound. And so do impossibilities.

RESPONSE

Where do you spend time outside the home and church during the week? Ask God to bless those places, the people in them and the activities pursued there. Pray that you might be alert to God's presence with you there and quick to respond to his promptings.

Day 12

Hope beyond our lifetime

READING

"Then all the people who were at the gate, along with the elders, said to Boaz, 'We are witnesses. May the Lord make the woman who is coming into your house like Rachel and Leah, who together built up the house of Israel … through the children that the Lord will give you by this young woman, may your house be like the house of Perez, whom Tamar bore to Judah.' "

Ruth 4.11–12

REFLECTION

Often when I think about the future I think about next week, next year or maybe five years' time. I want the future to be bright but not too far away.

The prayer that the people of Bethlehem pray for Ruth and Boaz is a prayer that the impact of their lives would continue for generations. The prayer is answered. Ruth and Boaz become the great-grandparents of the great King David. And so in turn the direct ancestors of Jesus. God answered their prayer but no one who prayed that prayer would have lived to see David crowned.

Yes, this is an encouragement to pray bold multi-generational prayers: for the great-grandchildren we will never see, or the regeneration of our town, or the transformation of our nation that may be a hundred years away. But it is also an encouragement to pray, like Adrian the teacher, for what we may never see ourselves: the conversion of a colleague who leaves, or of the mums and dads we'll lose touch with when our kids start going to different schools … We may not see them again but they will never be beyond God's gaze.

RESPONSE

Think about the next generation in your family. What would you like to see God do in and for and through them after you've died? Do the same for your local church.

the one about...
the
<u>stormtrooper</u>

Valeri Iliev trades in hope. He's a plumber. 6′ 3″, built like a rugby player. The only thing wider than his shoulders is his smile. He walks into every job with that smile on his face. Initially, at least, the smile can be a little confusing to his clients – not surprisingly perhaps. After all, they have water coming through the ceiling, and this giant of a man is smiling. Still, as he tells them, "I'm here now, it's going to be OK." He's a hope-bringer. It's not just that he has the skill to deal with whatever comes his way, it is that he brings calm, confidence, peace into the situation. And an alertness to the people he serves – their emotional, physical, mental, spiritual state.

A month ago, the company he works for expanded into TV-installation and he found himself in the flat of a man in his 70s. The flat was full of *Star Wars* memorabilia. And he commented on it to the owner who it turned out had helped design the first stormtrooper. They talked for a while and as the conversation went on Val noticed a passing look of anguish on the man's face.

"Are you alright?"

"No," the man replied, "I've been diagnosed with lung cancer."

"I'm sorry to hear that. I wonder, would you mind if I prayed for you?" Val asked.

"I'm not sure where I am with God these days," the man said.

And Val replied, "Wherever you are with God, I can tell you that God loves you, and that he's for you."

And so they prayed. And, as Val left, there was peace in the man's eyes.

Hope kindled. ●

Day 13

Hope beyond our faith – almost

READING

"And they brought the boy to Jesus. When the spirit saw him, immediately it threw the boy into convulsions, and he fell on the ground and rolled about, foaming at the mouth. Jesus asked the father, 'How long has this been happening to him?' And he said, 'From childhood. It has often cast him into the fire and into the water, to destroy him; but if you are able to do anything, have pity on us and help us.' "

Mark 9.20–22

REFLECTION

It's easy to assume that the future will be like the present but more so. If things are good, things will get better. If things are bad, things will get worse: the boss will never change; the school gate will always be snipey, gossipy, whingy; our football teammates always a bit too fond of a bit too much alcohol, always a bit too prone to crossing the line from banter to attack.

Take Denise's office. The atmosphere had always been backbitey, petty, acidic. Tough in a big organization, worse in a small office. Denise wondered if it could ever change. She prayed. And then, because she often got in before anyone else, she decided to play worship music and sing and pray.

To pray is to kindle hope. It had seemed impossible but, slowly, the atmosphere in the office changed, relationships improved, things got better.

When the boy's father says to Jesus, "If you are able to do anything ..." Jesus replies, "If you are able! – All things can be done for the one who believes." The boy's father responds, "I believe; help my unbelief!" Our hope lies not in how big our faith is but how big the God is in whom our mustard seed of faith nestles.

RESPONSE
Is there something in your life at home, at work, in the community that is not as you know God would like it to be but that you can't ever see changing for the better? Bring it to your heavenly Father in prayer, and ask him for his help.

Day 14

The hope that we bring...

READING

"As he approached the gate of the town, a man who had died was being carried out. He was his mother's only son, and she was a widow; and with her was a large crowd from the town. When the Lord saw her, he had compassion for her and said to her, 'Do not weep.'"

Luke 7.12–13

REFLECTION

Whenever Jesus enters a situation, new possibilities abound. In this instance, a woman, not only emotionally (and in all probability economically) devastated by the death of her husband, suffers the terrible agony of losing her only son, and so, in effect, provision for her old age. Humanly, the situation is hopeless.

But not for Jesus.

Resurrections or divine resuscitations are rare, though people do still give testimony of such occurrences.

What is less rare is God bringing hope into all kinds of situations. And often through his people. After all, whenever someone with Christ's Spirit enters a situation, new possibilities abound. We not only have hope, we are called to carry that hope into our day out in the world ... as Valeri does.

Yes, we live in the certainty that in Christ there is life after death but we also know that he cares now, and may choose to act supernaturally, or indeed through our words and prayers and actions that carry the fragrance of beyond and bring hope to those around us.

RESPONSE

Is there someone you know who is in particular need of encouragement today? What small thing could you do for them? A text? A prayer? A card? A cup of coffee on their desk? A Kit Kat? A knock on their door? Five minutes of your time?

Pray for them, too.

Hopeful faith, lovingly lived

WEEK 3

Reflections by Rachel Treweek

Day 15

Faith clothed in love

READING

"As God's chosen ones, holy and beloved, clothe yourselves with compassion, kindness, humility, meekness, and patience … Above all, clothe yourselves with love, which binds everything together in perfect harmony."

Colossians 3.12, 14

REFLECTION

Each day we choose what we are going to wear, and in some households people are making that choice for others, too.

For some people the choice in the daily decision about clothing may be reduced due to the necessity of a uniform. For others there is more freedom, and the choice of clothes is likely to be affected by the various tasks and events of the day.

The next story of everyday faith comes from Gem and is sparked by a party invitation. The wider story of Sarah's party will have involved friends choosing what to wear to Sarah's party, and for some of them this might have been quite time-consuming and even a source of anxiety amid an awareness of how easily we can be judged by our clothing. However, rather than focusing on the external appearance of Gem, Sarah and their friends, this snippet of story directs our eyes to Gem's "inner clothing" and her attitude towards Sarah.

In Gem's final decision to attend Sarah's party we see something of Gem's endeavour to "put on love".

RESPONSE

How do you hope people will respond to what you are wearing today, whether from choice or necessity?

Reflect on what "clothing yourself with love" might look like to those you encounter today in the different places where you will be.

the one about...
<u>the</u> party

"I hope you can come," Sarah said, handing Gem a pink and blue envelope. "Oh, thanks," said Gem brightly, but her heart sank. A birthday party invitation, the ninth of the year. At 11 years old there are a lot of parties and Gem had been to almost all of them. She liked parties, on the whole, and had only missed a couple for family reasons. But she didn't really get on with Sarah. Nothing deep – they just didn't click. Actually, Sarah wasn't that popular in the class. In fact, it was worse than that. Sarah wasn't particularly liked. Gem thought she might give this one a miss.

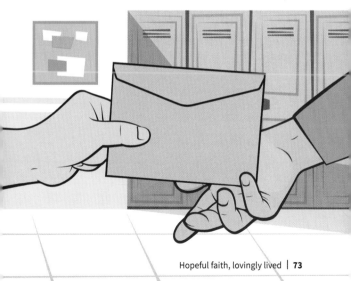

Still, over the next few days, Gem began to have second thoughts. Pretty much everyone in the class had been invited, and, as far as she could tell, not many were planning on going. Gem began to feel uneasy, and more so as she talked to other classmates.

She prayed about it. And it became clear to her what she had to do. "I wouldn't like it if no one came to my party. And I know God says that I am meant to be kind to others." She knew how strangely competitive parties were, and remembered feeling nervous that not many people would come to hers – though lots did. So, she told Sarah that she'd be there. And she told other people in the class that she would be going. And, as is sometimes the way of these things, and as a result of her example, quite a few of her classmates also decided to go along.

And the party was OK. And Sarah's dignity was protected.

Sometimes one person making a stand for compassion, setting aside personal preference, looking out for the best interests of another, can turn the tide, change a class, a team, a workplace, a family. ●

Day 16

Love is all you need

READING

*"I do not occupy myself with things
too great and too marvellous for me.
But I have calmed and quieted my soul,
like a weaned child with its mother;
my soul is like the weaned child that is with me."*

Psalm 131.1–2

REFLECTION

I suspect that most of us would say that we want
to do our bit in making the world a better place
and that we endeavour to show love in the way
we behave towards those around us. However,
if we're honest, those actions and words perceived
as love by other people are sometimes driven by
our brokenness. For example, sometimes we are
unhealthily motivated by a need to be needed,
or a desire to succeed or to be seen as special.

In the story about the party we catch a glimpse
of some of the dynamics between the friends

and of Gem's thinking behind her decision. While we can only speculate about Sarah's motivation for inviting people to a party, we can pause to reflect on how the story might have been different if Gem had craved her friends' affirmation and been driven by a desire to impress them in order to feel loved.

Our genuine love towards the people and places around us begins with receiving God's love in a place of complete dependence. God, like a perfect mother, longs to draw us close, to hold us and love us not because of who we are or what we've done but simply because we are a child of God.

RESPONSE

At one or two different points during the day make the choice to be still to acknowledge God's presence and receive God's love amid the concerns of your day.

Does this in any way transform how you seek to show love to the people in your day?

the one about...
Alive 107.3

`107.3`

Imagine you're 15 years old – that may take some doing. Your name is Niamh. You're in a Roman Catholic secondary school, in Glasgow, in the middle of a design and technology class, working on an exam project. You ask the teacher if he can put on some music.

The YouTube version of Reckless Love pops up on the screen.

You've never heard music like this before. And you ask your teacher, Mr Newton, "What kind of Catholic are you?"

The following week, Mr Newton (who is, in fact, a Baptist), puts on some music from Alive 107.3, a Dumfries Christian radio station. Then the DJ says, "A big shout for Niamh and all of you in Mr Newton's Design and Technology class at Caledonia Catholic High working on your exams. Keep at it, Shona, Jimmy, Caitlin, Jimmy, Graeme, Ruth, Sheila, Jimmy … This one's for you." Or words to that effect. And on comes I Am They's version of The King of Love my Shepherd is.

Imagine you're one of those pupils. You are never going to forget it – your name on the radio! The thoughtfulness, the creativity, the honour, the supportiveness. And those pupils couldn't wait to tell their friends, some downloaded it, played it to parents, one to the deputy head …

I don't know how God will use that action but I love that story precisely because none of us could copy it. It's so specific to that context: just for those particular students, just from that particular teacher.

And I love it because of what it says about the depth of loving concern that Mr Newton has for the pupils God has given him, a loving concern that's led him to such proactive creativity. ●

Day 17

Generous love

READING

*"There they gave a dinner for Jesus. Martha served,
and Lazarus was one of those at the table with him.
Mary took a pound of costly perfume made of pure
nard, anointed Jesus' feet, and wiped them with her hair.
The house was filled with the fragrance of the perfume."*

John 12.2–3

REFLECTION

Each day we live with assumptions about how things
will be, and there are unspoken norms about the
conduct expected of us in the places and activity of
our everyday lives. We are therefore shocked when
we encounter people in public or private spaces acting
in ways we would call "inappropriate". Such behaviour
or words often provoke people to turn their heads,
whether towards the activity or away from it because
it has been unsettling in some way.

The story of Mr Newton and his Design Technology class
is very different from the account in John's Gospel of

Mary anointing Jesus, but the events in the classroom still involved surprise, challenged assumptions and no doubt sparked a range of reactions.

Mr Newton's unexpected music and then the shout out from the radio DJ the following week became a catalyst for conversation, discussion and questions that rippled out beyond the classroom. While we don't know what emerged from all of this, we do know that it was rooted in Mr Newton's love and care for his pupils and his desire to challenge people's assumptions about Christ and his followers.

RESPONSE

As you go about your life today, identify an opportunity to do something potentially subversive: something that challenges assumptions of what would be expected at that time or in that place and which is about demonstrating generous love.

Day 18

Love transforming the ordinary

READING

"One of them, a lawyer, asked Jesus a question to test him. 'Teacher, which commandment in the law is the greatest?' He said to him, ' "You shall love the Lord your God with all your heart, and with all your soul, and with all your mind." This is the greatest and first commandment. And a second is like it: "You shall love your neighbour as yourself." ' "

Matthew 22.35 –39

REFLECTION

The worldwide communities of L'Arche were established by Jean Vanier. L'Arche communities involve people with and without learning disability living out their lives together and being transformed by each other, even amid the routine of daily living. Many people have been inspired and changed by the life of these communities which reflect Jean Vanier's words: "We are not called by God to do extraordinary things, but to do ordinary things with extraordinary love."

Joining in with the bringing in of the kingdom of God is about how we live every moment of the day including all that we consider ordinary and perhaps even mundane. This is about our hearts and minds as much as it is about our words and actions. And it is as much about those things we do that are unseen by anyone as it is about our visible behaviour in our encounters with other people.

RESPONSE

As you walk through today, whatever it holds, identify two or three things that you consider to be ordinary.

How might they be lived in a way that gives glory to God and reflects the values of the kingdom of God?

the one about...
minding
<u>the</u> gap

Remmie works for London Underground in customer support, interacting with thousands of customers each day. Imagine the stress. Busy people. People lost in a strange city. Tired people. People who have had a bit too much …

That's just the normal stuff, so imagine the stress when the temperature goes up and the signals go down. "When things go wrong," Remmie says with a smile, "the public go bananas." Remmie can't cool the day down or fix the track. But he can soothe the complaints and reassure people that the problems are being worked on. But that's not all. Remmie has to find a way to keep people moving. And he's found a way – he's got knowledge.

Remmie has to know his stuff. Knowledge of the Underground and knowledge of what is above ground. You see, people don't always know where they are going, and when travel is disrupted an alternative route needs to be plotted. And that isn't easy. Even then, once a way onward has been found, Remmie needs to know how to calmly move people on.
To keep them moving and keep cool even when this journey has got stuck.

You might think then when things go wrong that he's running through his mental map of the transport lines. Thinking through tricky questions he's had before, and how he answered them. You'd be right, he's got that knowledge. This isn't the knowledge, though, that Remmie says he relies on.

There's a gap, you see, between knowing what to say and then knowing how to say it. Remmie has a different knowledge to help here: the Psalms. He's learned many of them by heart, and when faced with a tricky spot it's a psalm that will spring to mind. That's what gives him courage to be firm or triggers an instinct of what to suggest. ●

Day 19

Rooted and grounded in love

READING

"I pray that, according to the riches of his glory, he may grant that you may be strengthened in your inner being with power through his Spirit, and that Christ may dwell in your hearts through faith, as you are being rooted and grounded in love."

Ephesians 3.16–17

REFLECTION

Throughout our day things are often changing. Sometimes that is the people we are with – both known and unknown; and sometimes it is the places where we are, whether for a few brief moments or several hours, depending on our daily tasks, work and leisure. In all of this we will be constantly reacting, consciously and subconsciously, to the present moment of people and place as our thoughts and emotions shift.

In Remmie's story we encounter someone who is constantly having to respond to numerous people in busy and ever-changing situations on the London Underground. While Remmie has to draw quickly on his knowledge and experience as he aims to answer people's questions, keep them calm and keep them moving, he is also clear that his rootedness in the Old Testament prayers of the Psalms enables him to draw on God's love and wisdom which he hopes is then reflected in what he says and how he says it.

RESPONSE

Amid the changes of today punctuate your time with small pauses to breathe deeply and look inwards as you open yourself once more to God's inner strengthening through the power of the Holy Spirit.

In these moments imagine your roots going deep into the soil of God's love. How might this affect what emerges from you in the way you engage with the people, places and tasks of the day?

Day 20

New every morning

READING

*"The steadfast love of the Lord never ceases,
his mercies never come to an end;
they are new every morning;
great is your faithfulness."*

Lamentations 3.22–23

REFLECTION

It is not unusual for the events of yesterday to impinge on today, particularly if they have left us feeling sad, disappointed, anxious, angry or frustrated.

It is also true that most of us are extremely capable of giving ourselves a hard time as we recognize the fact that we have sinned in "thought and word and deed, through negligence, through weakness and through our own deliberate fault … "

In Remmie's story of interacting with people on the London Underground he is being a transforming presence, yet there will inevitably be times not only when he is shocked or angered by things passengers say to him, but also times when he will wish that he had said something different or reacted differently. Yet the truth is that each day brings new opportunities for each of us, not least in receiving God's love and mercy afresh.

Today we are invited once more to enter into God's transforming work of reconciliation, and to open our inner eyes and ears to the possibilities of this day. This might, of course, mean living reconciliation in word and action in the light of yesterday, or it might mean letting something go so that we can move on.

RESPONSE
Take some time today to be aware of the places within you that need Christ's forgiveness and healing touch of love.

As you think about the people and places of your life today is there one thing, whether large or small, that you might live differently?

Day 21

Faith, hope and love ... every day

READING

"So if anyone is in Christ, there is a new creation: everything old has passed away; see, everything has become new! All this is from God, who reconciled us to himself through Christ, and has given us the ministry of reconciliation … So we are ambassadors for Christ, since God is making his appeal through us …"

2 Corinthians 5.17–20

REFLECTION

Living out our faith in everyday life is an invitation to find and follow God in a richer way. But we have an even richer invitation: God invites us to be Christ's ambassadors. To represent Christ in the places we spend our time, with the people we work with, share a home with or simply meet.

Remmie talks about how his faith is important in his role with his customers. He sees his job as service, to serve the public and look after them. However, Remmie has found another connection. It's in this service that he can also seek to be an ambassador for Christ. As he puts it, "Being an ambassador means remembering that people see your faith through the way you live your life."

The aim of these reflections has been to help us to find God in our everyday life and to think through how we follow God in the everyday. God has formed each of us to fulfil our calling to be ambassadors in different ways. Like Mike as a peacemaker, Gabi as a cool head in crisis or Gem's gift of compassion. As the Trenemans remind us, though, God is with us on this adventure. Nudging as we notice. As we live out our faith in hope and love maybe, just maybe, like Adrian we might hear God whisper that our small act of kindness or prayer has been noticed.

RESPONSE

Think back over the last 21 days – what's been the highlight for you? What have you learned about your calling as an ambassador?

If you've been doing this with a group or as a church, why not have a time to share these stories, *The one about …*?

Going further

We hope that these 21 days have been a fruitful time in helping you to notice where God is to be found in your everyday life – at school or in your home; with colleagues at work; waiting for a bus or a doctor's appointment.

We also hope that in this time you have a greater sense of what following God – being a disciple of Jesus – looks like in your everyday life. Whether this is a greater sense of calling or vocation or identifying the small acts of service that help you to witness to God's love.

But what next?

Here are three things we think you might be interested in doing.

To continue your journey

… why not look at some of the resources for living our whole lives for Christ produced by LICC? These can be found at **www.licc.org.uk/about/life**

These include an introduction to how God works in and through us in our everyday lives called *Fruitfulness on the Frontline*, written by Mark Greene. For those looking for resources specifically about working life, Mark's book *Thank God's it's Monday* is a good place to start.

To journey more with others into everyday faith

… why not introduce your church to a range of ways that together you can learn how to be churches that nurture everyday faith? Through a companion resource to these reflections – *Everyday Faith for Churches*. This booklet has seven small steps that your church leadership or PCC might try to help encourage everyday faith. You can download this for free at **www.churchofengland.org/everydayfaith**

For small groups you might also try LICC's *Life on the Frontline* offers six sessions – each with a short film, biblical reflections, real-stories and interactive exercises – to help small groups explore together Christ's call and commission to find and follow Christ in our everyday lives.

To deepen prayer for your everyday life

… why not download the prayer apps from the Church of England and make this part of your day-to-day routine? You might also like the series of Pocket Prayers, including: *Pocket Prayers for Commuters*, *Pocket Prayers for Work* and *Pocket Prayers for Troubled Times*. Apps and booklets are both available from Church House Publishing: **www.chpublishing.co.uk**

Most of all, keep talking – keep talking to your fellow Christians about how you are noticing God at work in your life, and the difference it is making Sunday to Saturday; keep talking to God whose spirit is with you wherever you go, alongside you with whoever you meet.